The Process

The Fun and Easy Way to Build an Income Stream for Life

Todd Burrier

Copyright © 2010, 2017 by Todd Burrier

Published by BalanceProfessor, LLC , Westminster MD

4th Edition September 2017

Printed by CreateSpace

Visit my blog:

www.toddburrier.com

Contents

Introduction

Dear Fellow Network Marketer,

I am so happy that you are holding this book in your hands because it means that you have heard from someone, probably a friend or business acquaintance, that network marketing is a wonderful way to develop an income stream for life. Even better is that you've either already taken the simple step to get started or you are seriously evaluating getting started (and probably struggling with the idea that this seems too simple). The first thing I want you to know is that your friend is telling you the absolute truth. I am living proof and so are many other people just like me. When I say "just like me" I am referring to people who started from humble beginnings, struggling to make ends meet, feeling like they were stuck in a rut, not doing the things in life they really want to be doing, and _____ (you can fill in your own blank).

You see, If you just met me and you looked at my credentials and my current station in life (I have an MBA, I have written books, I am a corporate leadership trainer, I sit on a few highly regarded boards in my community, I am an adjunct professor at various colleges, I live in a nice home, etc.), you might assume that it would be easy for me to build a business because I have credibility. What you need to know is that my current station is as a *result* of my success with network marketing.

When I began working with network marketing, I was someone who viewed himself as a failure in life. I had little business credibility. I was broke, shy, and suffered from very low self-esteem. *all* of the things I listed above came through my experience and success with this simple concept.

All I had going for me when I started this business, is that I am basically a nice person, and I am honest. Since I am by nature non-confrontational, selling and pressure tactics are not something I ever liked or would ever do (and fortunately they are counter-productive in this business). I was blessed to have found a business where the only requirements are being nice, honest, and sincerely trying to create a better life.

By the way, I call this a business, because the fruit of the effort is similar to the fruit of the effort of any business (profits). But I hate calling it a business because it is so different from what most people think of when they say the word "business." This is about relationships, helping people, fun, personal growth, investing in others, and yes, it also leads to an income stream and it can eventually be a huge income stream if you desire, but the truth is, if you do this the way it is supposed to be done….it doesn't feel like a business because it is so much fun.

This leads me to the next thing I want to make sure you are clear about. You already possess all that you need to succeed at the highest levels of network marketing. You are unique. You have your own set of natural talents, gifts, passions, and inclinations. You also have your own set of experiences and knowledge that you have accumulated in life. Becoming the best *you* possible is all that is required. You do not need a specific set of skills, training, education, upbringing, or anything else for that matter. You already have all you need to begin, and you can learn the rest as you go.

At this moment you are only months away from a passive style income (I'll explain this later) of $300-$500 per month. You are 3-5 years, part-time, from having a serious life-changing income stream. Maybe a little sooner if you are lucky and maybe a little longer if you are unlucky (I've never had luck in business, and have had to work hard for everything I've ever gotten). This concept requires no luck, you simply work "the process" over and over and in time you will reach the goal you want.

"The process" is simply the easy steps that create the cycle of customers and partners that build the business. The rest of this little book is about how to be immensely successful using this process. As you go through this information, you might say at some point "Could this possibly be all there is?" I won't blame you for thinking it. This is so simple that it is hard to believe it can be true. But it is. Most of the best things in life *are* simple. It is people who are complicated, and who try to complicate things.

The people like me who have a large network based income stream, simply work the process until they succeed. They don't question if it works. Think for a moment about the process of farming. Every year the farmer follows the same process; prepare the soil, plant the seed, nourish and protect the crop during the growing season, and harvest when the time comes. They know their process works, and they just work it. Yes, the results can vary based on many factors, but the underlying process works all the time. The same is true for the network marketer and the process you will learn in this book. They know for certain that the process works and they just work it. What is unknown for certain is who will work the process *with* us. That's the beauty of the process. It uncovers those who are ready to work in it and live a better life. There is nothing fancy about it. Anything is possible for you if you absorb this information and then live it. Incidentally, you can build any business in any industry with the core concepts in this book; you would just need to make the modifications necessary to fit your industry model.

The Need is Great

The first thing you've got to know is that the need is great. What I mean by this is simply, that almost everyone you talk to has a need that your offering can help with. There are 3 specific needs that the right network marketing company will address in the marketplace. The first 2, solutions based products/services and income are foremost in people's minds and represent needs they are actively thinking about solving. The third need is to have healthy relationships in all areas of life, which is a natural element of the network marketing world.

We live in a world where there is an ever increasing proactive approach to finding product and services solutions. We are an information based society where instead of simply waiting for a television commercial or magazine advertisement to tell us what to buy to solve a need or desire, we are searching on our own and open to new products and ideas. Because demand for quality continues to increase purchasing through word of mouth is at an all-time high.

Common dreams in these times

The need for people to find additional sources of dependable income is also great. Each day opens people's eyes to the reality that depending on a job as your future financial security is a dangerous bet. The only way to have financial security is to have a measure of control, and a home based network marketing income stream provides this. The needs vary from retirement funds, college/university funds, to simply needing more money to do the things that people want to do. A home based income stream is the perfect way to create an alternate source of income because it requires little to no investment of financial resources to develop, you can create it at your own pace, you can ultimately grow it as large as you'd like, and it is passive/residual in nature as it grows.

Passive/residual style income is income that does not require your direct effort to create it. Most people are familiar with the concept of exchanging time for money. You work for an hour and you receive a wage. If you don't work, you don't earn. This is called linear income and for our purposes, active income. Network marketing income starts as active income in that you are finding customers and teaching others to do the same, to derive your income. Over time however, people continue to reorder, when you have no involvement in this taking place. At this point your income is becoming passive style income.

With network marketing the income becomes more like royalty income. For example, an author writes a book once, but each time it is sold, they receive a royalty income. It could be 20 years after they wrote the book. In network marketing, when you have a network that purchases direct from the company, you can be paid each time they place an order even though you only were involved in the initial order. There is a little more to it than that, but this is the idea. If you develop a large base of people using your product and telling others about your product, you begin to derive passive style income in that it comes in every month regardless of how many new people you are introducing. This is the kind of income which allows you to have time freedom in your life should you decide to build it to a great enough level.

Different manner to earn money

Active income

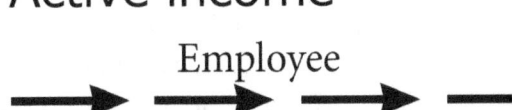

Employee

Month Month Month Month

Residual income

(over years)

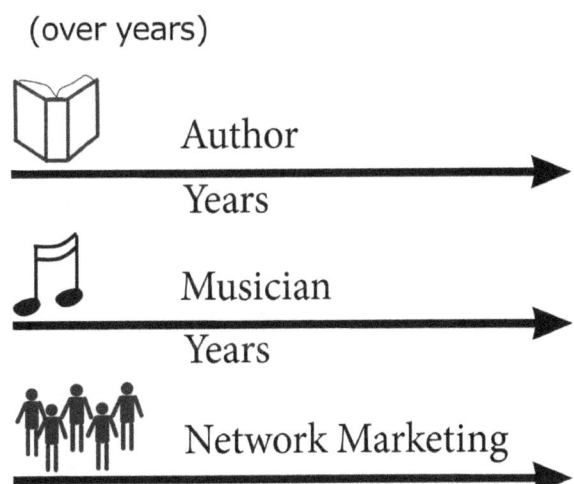

Author

Years

Musician

Years

Network Marketing

Years

The third need is something that all human beings require for a positive life experience. Human beings are relational creatures. We enjoy being around other people, especially people that add value to us or make us feel good. The people who participate in network marketing tend to be positive, motivated, forward thinking people who genuinely care about others and desire to make a difference. In essence they are a community of encouraging and positive people who enjoy helping people (hmmm, I wonder if your work/job environment is like this...). The very core concept of network marketing is to help others first, knowing that if you help enough people get what they need in life, you will get what you need.

Your Obstacles

Building your business is simple and the process of doing it is easy, but that doesn't mean it will be free of obstacles. The minute you decide to pursue any goal in life, there are things that will stand in your way. This is true of deciding to walk across a street as much as it is to pursuing a big project. *The bigger the goal the greater the obstacles.* Naturally, your decision to build a lifetime income through network marketing will have obstacles, but they can be overcome in time. You will have three primary obstacles: Patience with self, time utilization and focusing on serving other's first.

Time utilization will be the first challenge to overcome. Today's modern lifestyle is fast-paced and everyone feels busy. You will be putting your new pursuit into your already busy life. A key feature of the network model is that your partner company does most of the time consuming elements (paperwork, tracking processing and shipping orders, etc.). All you have to do is communicate with people the proper way to facilitate the development of the business. This can be done online and offline in as little as a few hours per week and you will have mentors helping you structure your time to best work with your schedule. This is an easy challenge to overcome, because this is an easy business to fit into your life.

Having patience with yourself is a little more challenging and will be directly affected by how big of an income you desire to create and how personally developed you currently are. You will be learning and personally growing through the process, but it will be natural for you to want to be an expert in all aspects of your venture immediately. Expertise takes time to develop and is a product of repetition, which comes from doing the business over time. The only way to learn is by doing, but fortunately the process is designed such that expertise is not needed in order to succeed.

I will show you the steps to succeed, and you will gain expertise as you go. The rare time you need a higher level of information or know-how you will have mentors along side of you to step in and provide it for you. This will make more sense to you as you discover the ease of the process. The other area of patience is the natural desire to want instant success. There is nothing of lasting value that happens overnight. The quick success view in life is the downfall of many people in many things (I learned this the hard way!).

Follow the teaching and you will gradually develop an income for life. Ignore the teaching and try to short-cut the process and you will still be looking for the magic solution 20 years from now.

The biggest challenge you will face is focusing on others first. It is normal human instinct to think about ourselves first. When you share your offering with someone else it is natural to think about how great it would be to have them get involved because it would be good for you. This is a major mistake. People can sense when you are trying to sell them for your own benefit. *Never do this*. Remember the need is great.

Your focus must be on allowing the other person to learn how your products or your network model can help them meet their need. Their decision to meet their need is not about you-it is entirely about them. You are simply the messenger. This takes the pressure off of both of you. Your purpose is only to share how good this is and let the process uncover those who are ready to act on their needs at the time they are ready to act. The philosophy is to help enough other people get what *they* need and then you will get what *you* need. As you will see, the process works-you only have to do the process and the right people will step forward at the right time.

Perhaps you are wondering why I did not mention fear as an obstacle. The reason is simple. I don't want you to give fear too much credit as something that is truly in your way. Of course fear is a real thing, but in the sense of working something as fair and good as network marketing, the fears are common fears that are inherent in most new encounters. The fears that would hold you back from building a network income are learned fears that are overcome by taking action. These fears are fear of failure, criticism, and rejection. We are not born with a pure fear of these things.

Consider the way a child learns. Everything from learning to stand and walk and then run, to riding a bike, skiing, and skating, to reading, writing and mathematics, is a series of learning through failing. Children do not fear failure. They naturally try and try and try until they finally do the thing they are trying to do and then they try something else. They keep going because it is not in their mind that they cannot do it.

Children do not naturally fear criticism until they are criticized. When they are young their parents simply encourage them and they keep trying. As they get older and the number of influences in their life expands, this is when people start to criticize them for what they are doing. This experience is emotionally painful and they begin to attempt to avoid this. This is where fear of criticism develops.

Fear of rejection is also a purely learned response. How many times will a child ask you for a cookie? As many times as it takes! You may say no 20 times, but they will keep asking, and eventually they will get a cookie. It is generally understood that not everyone will say yes, regardless of what you are doing. The bigger aspect of the fear of rejection is the personal side. This is the fear that someone will think less of you or different of you because you are doing something they may not agree with. The old adage is that *if someone is not up on it, they are down on it.* All people who have accomplished something above average in life have had *many* others tell them that it couldn't be done. The bigger the thing that was accomplished, the more people there were who said it couldn't be done! This is normal. Here are a few things to consider; *if someone truly thinks less of you because you are doing something to help yourself and to help others, is this really the kind of person whose opinion you should care about?*

The right kinds of people, the kinds of people you want in your life, will have a new higher level of respect for you because you are aspiring to accomplish something. This is the point of why this fear is misguided. Instead of fearing who might think less of you, be excited about all the quality people who will now think *better* of you. Or, if you can, treat people well, work at growing your business, and don't worry about what other people think. Because the truth is that other people aren't spending their time in life thinking about you, they are thinking about themselves!

All things of value in life will require having to learn and try over and over. All things of value in life will subject you to the opinions of others. These will be criticisms (although what they truly are is the other person's ignorance and self-limitations projected on to you-so don't be upset with them, instead feel sad for them because this is hurting *their* quality of life). All things of value in life will involve people and circumstances telling you no. To fear these things would mean you have not learned these lessons yet. This means that you have already missed out on many things in life because of this fear (I missed out on many things in my life before I learned this lesson). This leads to the pain of regret when you later realize that you could have done what you feared. The pain of regret lasts a lifetime. Fear goes away when you take action upon the thing that you fear. You will get nothing you desire in life if you always run from fear. The process I will teach you in this book deals with very little rejection and very little criticism, as you will see. Therefore, to fear these will be simply stopping yourself from gaining the fruit that is available for you to pick.

One last thought on the idea of fear and it's probably the most valuable thing I could give you. *Fear in this process means we are being self-centered!* Yes, you read this over-emphasized statement correctly. You can only have fear if you are thinking about yourself. If you are worried what they might say, or what they might think about you, or if they might say no to you…these thoughts are all about you (once I grasped this truth, it made it easy to talk to people).

The key to this process is that it is all about them. You are simply giving someone an opportunity to better their life. You are giving them a gift! If they choose not to do so, this is their choice and you need to respect it and understand that you have done what you are supposed to do. Therefore, if you ever feel fear when you are about to talk to someone, remember this and focus on them.

Behavior Keys

Treating people right in life is always the right thing to do on a personal level, and is a necessity to having good relationships. There is also a practical aspect when it comes to business. People *want* to do business with people they like and they will *only* do business with people they trust. Of course this assumes that you are providing something of value that is competitive in the market place. I have built my business on this very foundation. The behaviors that are important to demonstrate for long term success are kindness, honesty, and respect. The principles within these behaviors that you need to display are serving the other person's needs before your own, and never pressuring anyone. As you will further understand during the process explanation, this set of behaviors and principles is most important during the business process for two very specific reasons.

The first reason is that people need to feel comfortable and at ease before they are receptive to learning. Ours is not a process of convincing. The need is great for product solutions and financial solutions. People do not need to be convinced that they need solutions. They simply need to feel comfortable enough to explore your offer to see if it is a solution they would choose. Therefore, ours is a process of simply allowing them to discover what we have in a way that when they are ready to take action on solving their need, they will do so through our offering. If they feel that you are pressuring them or feel that you will pressure them, they will be focused on how to defend themselves and not on what you have to offer. The learning can only happen if they feel comfortable and safe. They need to know that they are free to choose, and if they choose not to take your offer at this time, that will be okay.

The second reason relates to how *you* will feel in the process. If the process is enjoyable, and fun, and fulfilling, you will work in the process as much as you can. It is human nature to continuously do things which we enjoy. Being in easy, comfortable communication with someone where the possible outcome is that they might do better in life and you might be part of making it possible? This feels amazing! You see, when you don't pressure the other person or try to convince them, it doesn't just take the pressure off of them-it also takes the pressure off of you. You have no need to worry about making a perfect presentation or saying the right thing at a certain time. You will simply be opening a door through a pleasant conversation. This is easy to do.

Not Yet

When you follow the process you are about to learn, keeping the behavior keys at the front of your efforts, you do not hear the word no. You only hear *not yet*. You already understand that the need is great. For the most part, everybody you speak with has a need that you can help them solve. The question is only are they ready to act on solving it yet. When you treat them properly and they say no, what they are truly saying is not yet, or not with you yet. Sooner or later, the need will reach a point where they will have to act, and by following the process with the right behaviors, you will be there when their time comes.

The only time the word no comes into play is if someone does not treat *you* properly. You are being nice and offering people an opportunity to help themselves. If they are cynical, you can respect this. If they are skeptical, you can respect this. If they are not ready to act on their need, you can respect this. But if they are mean, unfriendly, rude, disrespectful, or any other behavior you would like to place in this category…you do *not* have to respect this. You can say no to them. You can decide that they will no longer have the opportunity in the future to meet their need through you. In your workplace, you have to work with whoever your boss puts near you. This is your network marketing business. You can work only with who you want. There is no shortage of people who have a great need. Pick the nice ones.

The Process

Now it's time to learn the process of building a lifetime business to whatever level you care to grow it. This is easy to do. I don't mean easy from the standpoint that you have to do very little to succeed. I mean easy from the perspective that the steps in this process are easy to actually do. Working for someone else your entire life is hard. Working in manual labor is hard. Working around people who are negative in an office environment you do not enjoy is hard. Working in a job that is not fulfilling and in which you are not passionate is hard. By comparison this is incredibly easy, but it does take consistent effort over a long period of time if you want to develop a large success. The process is simply a conversation that contains 4 simple steps that you repeat over and over:

Approach, Information, follow-up, and service.

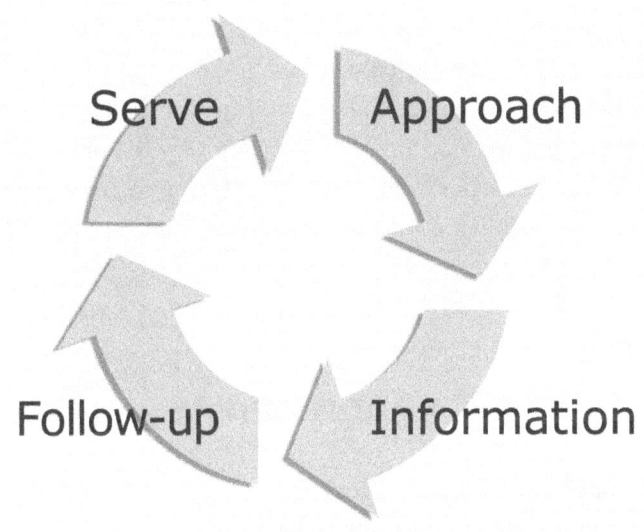

The conversation starts with the approach and it never ends unless you decide it does or if the person you are talking to is not nice. These steps are enjoyable if you follow the insights I give you here and you cannot fail if you do them as I teach them. You also need to understand that in order to be effective in the process you do not have to know every little thing about what you are offering. Your knowledge is not nearly as important as your behavior and your conviction.

Working *With* Human Nature

Human nature indicates that in general 20% of the people in communities and organizations tend to be the real doers. These people account for 80% of the productivity. Relating this time-tested reality to the process gives you a clear understanding of how to work with human nature. If 10 people have the same need, human nature tells us that only two are ready to act on that need right now. So if you know ten people who need what you have to offer, typically two are ready to act. The process allows you to sort through the ten comfortably and find the two. You don't try to convince the other 8 to act. They aren't ready yet. Trying to convince the other 8 is working *against* human nature. You simply use the process to find the two.

Approach

The approach, also called contacting, is the initial step where you are simply inviting someone to learn about what you have to offer. The first thing to grasp about the approach is that it is much less important *what* you say, as it is *how* you say it. Remember, the approach is simply the beginning of the conversation. Therefore, as you learned in the behavior keys, you need to be nice, honest, respectful, focused on serving the other person's needs, and absolutely no pressure. For you to fully grasp the power of this way of doing business I will show you a comparison between working with pressure versus working without pressure.

Pressure

Let's assume that you are approaching 10 people. If you are approaching with a hype-based pressure approach, 8 out of 10 people will not be interested in learning about what you have to offer. These will likely be the 8 who aren't ready to act, but that is not the point. You want the people you approach to have a positive experience with you and to learn about what is available for them because at some point in the future they will be ready to act.

People are sick of pressure tactics and using them will make you appear just like everyone else who has pressured them in the past. Regardless of how great their need is they will not want to talk with you when you approach with pressure, and they will not be open in the future to speaking with you. The even bigger thing to understand about this is that you did not just alienate these 8 people, but also everyone that they are close to. People talk to their closest friends and family about things they don't like. Negative news travels much faster and farther than positive news. These people will, on average, tell at least 10 people (probably more) about your unpleasant approach. This means that you now have alienated 80 additional people in your market place.

With pressure you also have to be saying the exact right thing at the exact right time because it is a form of manipulation. This puts pressure on you too. I remember when I first started in a networking business and the training was all around the pressure and hype approach. This made me so uncomfortable that I didn't want to work the business.

I tried doing it but I couldn't behave that way so I just talked to people nicely and openly and guess what? It worked!

Now 2 people still agree to learn about what you are offering. Why would they do this if you are pressuring? Because the need is so great that some people will agree to meet with you anyway even if you approach them the wrong way. You will more than likely, because of the law of numbers, have one of the 2 agree to participate in your offer because the need is so great and this person is at a place in their life where they are ready to act on their need and you came along at the right time. They will take your offer immediately because you are using pressure and immediacy is the nature of pressure, plus they are ready to act.

The other one will probably say no because you used pressure, and they will not want to speak with you again (same for their close contacts) about this because the experience of pressure is very unpleasant. So while you still got one to agree, you have now completely closed the door forever with about 100 people in the process. This is not a good business model for long term success in the community!

No Pressure

The no pressure approach is easy to do and yields a much greater initial result and long term result. When you approach the 10 people with no pressure and make them feel comfortable and safe to learn, 5-7 of these people will be willing to take the next step and learn about your offer. The people who say no to your approach, will still go into your pipeline (pipeline is a term for the people who are somewhere in your process. Even though these people said no initially, they are now in your process to be contacted at a later time). This is because your approach is pleasant and therefore does not permanently close the door for these contacts.

They will always remember that you were nice and did not pressure them, and will be open to you contacting them again in the future (and remember, things change in people's life. I remember one guy I called every 6 months for 4 years and he always said no (not yet), then one call, he said "I think I'd like to learn about it." I ended up sponsoring him. This happens *all* the time, and a lot of times people will eventually call me).

The immediate result of these conversations will be at least the same as the result with pressure and probably better. What I mean, is that the person who said yes with pressure will also say yes with no pressure, because they are ready to act on their need. In addition, there is a much greater chance that you will also involve at least one more immediately because they were ready to act on their need (human nature) but did not want to be pressured so they never even learned what was available! Recognize that each approach you make lets someone know that you are in business. Therefore, just the act of making the contact is a positive step for your future success and those that don't say yes to your offer after the approach will go into your pipeline for a later conversation and over time, you will involve more of these people. You will see how this happens as you learn the next steps in the process.

Making Them Comfortable

The key to the approach is to make the other person feel safe and comfortable to learn. This is done mostly through how you say what you are saying, but there are a few things that are important to communicate. You need to be authentic and real, not slick and polished. You need to be relaxed. No hype or exaggeration. These are signals to the other person who will be listening to you through ears that have been pressured before and will immediately put them on the defensive.

When you have a nice, relaxed, authentic approach this will immediately make them more at ease. During your invitation to learn about your offer it is important for you to say things like "if it's not for you that's okay" or "it might not be for you but that's' okay" or "I want you to know that it is fine by me if you say no at any time." You must help them realize that your intention is purely to have them learn about this wonderful thing that you have found and are benefitting from, because you think it might be something that they could benefit from (use the word "learn" when you are talking to them..."would you be open to learning about it?"). The major point is that you have found something you believe in and it could help them too, but if they don't see it that way you respect that. You simply want to make them aware of it and share information about it and they can do what they would like from that point forward. (For specifics on Approach, see Addendum 2)

Information

The approach finds out if someone is interested in learning about your offer. This information step is where they learn enough to know if they are truly interested in it at this time. While you will undoubtedly have access to several excellent information tools and presentation materials, the most effective thing you can share in this step is your story. I said previously that you do not have to know a lot about your offer, or have all the information about your offer, to be effective in helping people with your offer. I sponsored a lot of people before I knew most of the information about the products and marketing plan. Remember, the need is great. You simply have to allow the other person to feel that this could be an answer for them. That is the most important part, and at that point they will ask you to get them any information they require to make a decision.

This starts with your story. *The most successful people in network marketing are the people who tell their story the most.* A major misconception about a story is that people believe it has to be a big, dramatic story to be effective. Nothing could be further from the truth. As you will see the bigger and more dramatic a story is, the less another person can relate to it. The other thing to understand here is that when human beings listen to a story, they don't evaluate what is right or wrong with the story (as they do with a planned out presentation of information), they simply see the story in their own mind and become involved in it emotionally.

Perfectly mapped presentations designed to convince the other person position them to defend themselves and place a burden of proof on you. You have to be a master presenter to succeed with a pure presentation style. What I am teaching you will allow you to be more effective in the long run without ever having to be a master at presenting information. I will explain this as I outline the anatomy of a story.

1. The first thing in your story needs to be a description of what problem you were trying to solve. A problem by definition does not need to be negative (although most people interpret it this way). *A problem is anything you are trying to solve.* Wanting to have more energy is a problem, wanting to eat better is a problem, wanting to have enough money to retire is a problem, and wanting to own a home at the beach is a problem. So essentially solving a need or a desire is a problem by this definition. The key here is that everyone has problems they are looking to solve. The need is

great. The minute you share the problem you were trying to solve, the other person can begin relating to you and thinking about what problems they would like to solve. Everyone listens to everything from the perspective of "what's in this for me." Sharing the problem allows them to begin thinking about how your solution might end up being their solution.

2. The next part of your story needs to be the journey you went on to solve the problem. Share the details of different things you tried that didn't work. How that made you feel. Do not shortcut this part because this is the fabric of the story. Think about a movie for example. In the first ten minutes you learn about the problem and the rest of the movie is all about the journey to solve it. The person you are telling the story to will relate to your efforts to solve their problem because they are presently in their own journey to solve their problem.

3. Now you share how you learned about this solution. This is where you introduce the idea that someone shared this with you while you were in your journey. It shows that another person sharing this was the key to you learning about it. What doesn't need to be said but is perfectly understood, is that at the moment you are sharing this aspect, you are sharing your solution with this person while they are in the middle of their journey.

4. Here is where you will share what you learned that made you think that this could be the answer to your

problem. The key points about your offer that make it so special are the things you want to talk about right here. This is a major moment of difference from a presentation of information. You see if you are giving a presentation and you say "and what makes our company so special is that we have this and this and this," you are simply providing information. But when you share how you felt when you learned about these special things it allows the other person to experience the feeling of discovery just as you did. At this time you can also share the story of the person who shared it with you which further creates possibility for the person you are speaking with. This is very powerful.

5. Your experience so far is the last thing you need to express. You can share a testimony about how it is making a difference for you. You can talk about how great the company is to work with. You can talk about all the great people you've met. You can share stories of people you've helped already. It's up to you. Just share your heart.

The beautiful thing about this is that this requires little training. It is simply the truth. You are purely sharing the truth and your experience with someone else. Anyone can do this and be effective. Once you have finished the story the other person will either be interested or not. If they are not interested at this time they will tell you no immediately. They will say no immediately because even though you have a no pressure approach, they are going to expect you to pressure them because of their past experiences in life. They don't want to be in a situation of pressure so they will say something like "that sounds good, but I don't think it's for me." If they say no, you simply thank them for their time and say something like "thanks for taking the time and getting together, is it okay if I check in with you every now and then to see how you are doing?" Most people will say yes.

The power to what just happened is that you said it would be okay if they aren't interested and then you kept your word. They will not forget this. The experience was enjoyable for them, because stories are fun to listen to and interesting. The other important point is that they will not forget the story, because unlike listening to information, which is all in the head, listening to a story is also emotional. When you allow them to say no, they will continue to think about what you said and wonder if they are missing out on something. This person then goes into your pipeline to contact at a later date, because 2 things are certain: the need is great and will remain so, and things in life change. Someone who does not think your solution is their answer today might think it is the only solution that makes sense tomorrow.

If the person says anything other than no, then they are interested at some level. The great thing is that they will ask you for whatever information they need. Perhaps they will want to know about the products, or the compensation structure, or how it works, or the history of the company. All of this is easily supplied, regardless of how new you are and you will also have other people helping you if you need it.

On rare occasion when you finish the story the other person is silent. Simply ask them if this is something they would like to learn more about. When they say yes, ask them what they would like to know. It is this simple. (For additional insights about the power of stories, see addendum 3)

Follow up

Follow up is simply the continuation of the conversation. This is where many people make the mistake of giving up too soon. We must always remember that the entire process is about the other person and not ourselves. We might believe that they should act immediately on their need, but it is up to them when they act on their need. It is our job to make sure that we are there when they are ready to act. Many people are hesitant to follow up consistently because they do not want the other person to feel like they are being pressured. This would only be true if you *were* pressuring them, which you will not be. You have already made it clear to your prospect that it is okay to say no to you at any time in the process. Therefore, you are simply doing what any good business person would do when you follow up.

If you do not follow up here is how you appear: You look like you don't care about them, you look like you don't really believe all the great things you shared with them, you look unprofessional, you look like this is not important, you look like you are not very serious about your business, etc.

Follow up is part of all businesses. Your contact expects you to follow up. The majority of all business in the world is conducted after the 4th contact. If you do not follow up you will miss the majority of your opportunities to help people and hurt your chances of success. Even more importantly you will ruin your credibility with the prospect. Follow up is where the true success happens. Most of the people I have sponsored in my career have come through follow up. Sometimes it is the same day or week and sometimes it is months or years later. It doesn't matter how long it takes because it happens when it should if you work the process, and you will have plenty of people taking action to keep you busy while the others are working their way through your process as long as you put new people in your process everyday.

All you have to do is be nice and sincerely interested in answering their questions and providing information. The more you follow up, the more rapport you will develop, the more you will learn about them and their needs, the more they will believe you are the kind of person they would want to do business with, and the more your credibility will grow.

Always follow up with someone until they tell you no (not yet). At the point that they say not yet, you will simply put them in your Not yet file and contact them again in 3-6 months.

It is important to have a basic tracking system for your prospects. You can use an online type of contact manager or something as simple as an index card file. You want to make note of every piece of information they share with you about their life. This helps you build deeper rapport every time you speak with them and allows you to pick up the conversation where you last left it. For instance, if they share with you about something their kids are involved in or a situation with their work, you can ask about this the next time you speak. This is very powerful for continuing the rapport you had the previous time you spoke. Each time you speak, their trust in you grows. People do business with people they like and trust.

Serve

Once someone makes the decision to accept your offer, it becomes time for you to shine by serving them. Many businesses look at this stage of the process as the "close." While this is a completion of an initial purchase, it is really the beginning of a new level in your relationship. You have just moved into a partnership of sorts with this person. Now is the time to really focus on helping them because they have stepped forward and said "I want to help myself and I am trusting you to be the person to assist me in this."

If the person is choosing to become a customer of your offer, you need to ensure that they have the greatest experience possible with your product. You need to make sure they know all the ways to use it so that they will receive the benefit they are looking for. You need to provide the kind of ongoing service that makes them feel valued and cared about to such a level that they would never consider using a competitor's product because they would know that they would no longer have you in the equation. People become loyal to people before they become loyal to products. They will forgive a product mistake much easier than a service mistake. Think about a meal in a restaurant. If you have a dish that you are not happy with, but the service is excellent and you feel valued, you will likely go back. But if the food is good, yet the service is horrible and you don't feel valued, you will likely not return.

The minute they place an order for your product, you need to set a time to follow up when they receive the product so that you can personally walk them through their first experience. The same day you need to also send a hand-written thank you note. These two simple and easy things to do will separate you from almost everyone else they do business with. They will put you above everyone in the service world and make you unforgettable. They will also give the new customer the ultimate in confidence that they made a good choice and set the expectation that you are dependable and will be there for them. This is invaluable for your long term relationship.

From a practical standpoint, you will be ensuring that the customer's first experience is excellent. First experiences are the same as first impressions. They last a long time. An excellent first experience with your product will also ensure that they continue to use it and therefore ensure that the true benefits will be realized. This will lock the customer into you and your product for the long term and make your overall retention well beyond what most people experience in business.

You continue to serve the customer through adding value to their life through emailing information that would be helpful to them and calling every now and then to check in and see if they have any questions or needs. By maintaining a value added level of contact, when they have a need other than what you are currently serving, they will come to you because they are already in a trusting relationship with you. Whenever you have a new product or promotion you will be well received because of the trust, but If you *only* contact them with promotion of products you will be seen as only interested in making more money from them.

If someone has made the decision to join you in the business side of your offer, you will treat them the same way. The thank you note and the first experience are the same, with the exception that you will also begin training and mentoring them on how to do the process.

The first step would be to give them a copy of this book so they can understand how easy this is to work in. Then you would get together with them to make sure they understand what tools are available to them, that they know how to do the basic administrative things that might be necessary (like setting up a website, placing orders, where to find information, company contacts, etc.), review with them the compensation model so they understand how their future income will be created, and talk with them about their goals and action plan.

This is the most fun part of the business because now you are in the part of the process where you are truly an agent of helping people make a positive change in their life. Few things feel as good as helping people have a better life!

An important note here is that people will participate for a variety of reasons and to achieve various levels of success. Never consider what this person can do for you. Only focus on how you can serve them in achieving their goals and dreams. Every goal someone has is important to them, and therefore it should be important to you. It doesn't matter the size of the goal. It only matters that you help someone achieve it. You need to help your new partner understand that you are available for anything they need and that you will help them to whatever level they want.

The majority of people who join you in your business will want to achieve a modest level of financial success. An extra 300-500 dollars per month is an extra 3600- 6000 dollars per year. This is a serious improvement in lifestyle for 80% of the people in the developed world. Help enough people reach even modest goals and you can reach your grandest goals.

You will find people who want to do more than this and that will be fun too. There is no limit to what is possible in this concept. What is important to remember is the size of the goal does not determine the value of the person. Help everyone achieve whatever goal they have and you will have a very successful business that will pay you income for life.

A Few Closing Thoughts

I know you read through this quickly and now you might be sitting there thinking, "is this all there is?" Well, yes…and a little no. This is all there is to the process, but that doesn't mean you will automatically behave in the exact way you should or approach someone the perfect way. It's okay though, because you will immediately do better than someone who didn't read this book!

I suggest you read this book frequently the first month. Each time you read it you will be further into working the process and you will understand things in a new way. This is incredibly simple. It won't take you long to begin mastering the process and thriving in it, but there will still be a learning curve.

There will also be many things you will want to learn about the company and the products, etc. These will help you be more confident as time goes on, but remember it is not necessary to know this to be effective. Learn it as you go, but begin building immediately.

Remember, you are a unique and special creation. No one else is exactly like you. You have been blessed with all you need to succeed at the highest level.

You simply have to work the process and become the best *you* possible. You can absolutely create the life you want, and you can do it through network marketing. Life is shorter than you realize. Don't settle for less than you can be. Grab the reigns and go for it. I hope you have enjoyed this little book and I look forward to hearing from you down the road as your success grows. Please feel free to email me and let me know your progress.

Many Blessings,

Todd Burrier

Visit me at my blog:

www.toddburrier.com

Get my free audio training "27 Phrases that Really Work in Prospecting for Your Home Business."

Addendum 1 – A Business Building Philosophy

It is my goal and the responsibility of any mentor to give the person they sponsor into the business the best possible chance to succeed. The majorities of the people who get involved in your opportunity have never been successful in their own business before, and likely have never been in their own business before.

This means that not only do they have a lot to learn about their new venture, but they have a lot to learn about themselves too. It is crucial that when someone gets started, we help them to grow themselves and their business at the same time. My belief is that if you grow the person, the business will follow. But you must help that person realize that they can do it, for this to be possible.

There are many philosophies of building in the industry and all of them have merit. If someone is willing to do enough of anything they will eventually succeed. I am not attempting to make anyone else's philosophy wrong in this book. I am only sharing my own philosophy that has taken me years to grow into. I know for a fact that anyone can learn and succeed using the principles that I teach.

1% or 99%?

In my 28 years of networking experience, as well as my involvement and experiences in the community and working with corporations, I have reached the conclusion that about 1% of any population in any country has what I would call true business credibility. A person with true business credibility can call someone on the phone and tell the person that they would like to talk to them about a business and the other person immediately agrees, without question. This 1% includes people who have been successful in network marketing.

The other 99% of the population does not have this business credibility. Most of these people have never been in their own business before and those that have did not experience any measurable success. If someone from the 99% calls someone to say they would like to talk to them about a business they are likely to get a question like "What do you know about business?"

When someone joins your opportunity they are excited about the possibility of succeeding. But their belief that they will succeed is not nearly as high as their enthusiasm because they have not succeeded in business before, especially this kind of business before, and the chances are good that they don't know anyone who has succeeded either.

To give the new person the best chance to grow into a higher level of belief it is important to have them work in a way where they feel they are succeeding and developing. If I tell a 99% person to begin immediately recruiting for the business when they get started here is what happens. They call someone they know and tell them that they would like to talk to them about a business. The person says "What do you know about business?" This hurts their already low true belief that they can succeed. After 3 or 4 of these responses the person no longer believes that they can succeed and that their friends are right and this doesn't work.

I understand this pain and discouragement because this is where I was when I first started. I was a 99%er. I am adamant about giving anyone else who comes from the 99% the chance to grow into a 1%er if they want to.

Product belief is something that is not subjective. If someone has belief in what their products (or service) can do for people and they share that with someone, even if the other person is not interested, they cannot steal the person's product belief. So, if someone is coming from the 99% group and is uncomfortable approaching someone about the business possibility at first, they should start by focusing solely on developing their customer base.

Each customer someone sponsors helps them build their confidence, their belief in themselves, and their belief in the business and their ability to succeed in the business. By the time the new builder has several (I like them to have 15 or more) customers; they will be more comfortable to begin approaching for the business. This is because now they have built a successful little business that is producing positive cash flow. So when they call someone and say that they have a business they would like to talk to them about and the person asks them what they know about business they are able to say that they started a business that already has several customers. It is a simple process and anyone can do it. They are also in a position to teach someone else how to do what they have already done. This forms the basis for duplication in the business.

Addendum 2 – Approaches Tips, Words, and Ideas

There are many ways to talk to people. The key is to find something you are comfortable saying and then say it over and over. The right people will be interested as long as you are nice, honest, non-pressuring and respectful. The key to the business is sharing with as many people as possible.

This addendum is oriented towards making the approach by phone, but the words would be the similar if the approach was in person or via direct message/text. Below, in no particular order are various things I've said at different times in my career and all of them are effective. Remember, how you are saying what you say is even more important that what you say, but if what you say is good too, then you will be even more effective.

This section is purely business approaches. Addendum 4 is a bonus addendum for people who are working with health and wellness products.

The first thing you do is excuse the time when you call. You do this by asking if they have a minute to talk (or however you want to say it). This immediately sets a respectful tone to the call because you are being considerate. Then you would make your approach. A very effective method is to do what I call a "reach" via direct message/text and simply say something like "I'm trying to catch up with you, when can we talk for a minute?" or "Can you talk for a minute?" In many cases this will get you to a phone call much faster than calling and leaving a voicemail. Below are various things you can say in the main part of your invitation to learn.

To make them comfortable:

It's okay if it's not for you…

This might not be for you (and its okay if its not)…

You can say no any time and that's okay…

It might not be a fit for you…

Good stuff to say:

This is not like anything I've seen before…

If I could show you a way to make more money, without financial risk, would you be open to learning about it?

Are you open to a way to earn income?

Are you open to a side project where you could make some extra money?

I'm expanding my business and it might not be for you but you are exactly the kind of person I'd like to work with, would you be open to learning about what I'm doing?

I've started a business and I am looking for a few partners to run with me, there's no capital investment, would you be open to learning about it?

I found a great home business and I'm building a team, it might not be for you, but would you be open to learning about it?

I've found a unique home business concept that I'd like to run by you, are you open to a way to diversify your income?

I started a business that is perfect for today's economy and I'm looking for a few people to work with me, it's probably not for you but would you be open to learning about it?

I've found the fairest home business…

I've found the most honest home business…

I've been looking for a way to create more income for (retirement, college, etc.) and I found this incredible business with no risk that's all about helping people, would you be open to learning about it?

I've started a business and I am looking for the right person to work with, I thought of you. It might not be for you but would you be open to learning about it?

If I sent you some information about my new business would you look at it? If its not for you that's okay.

If I sent you a short video clip about my new business would you look at it?

I found a great home business that's fair and honest and all about helping people. I'm looking for a few people and I thought of you. Are you open to learning about a way to create another income stream?

These are two network oriented approaches (I teach an entire course on cultivating networks) that are very effective:

I'm expanding my business and I'm looking for a certain kind of person. I respect you and it seems that you might know some of the right people for me to talk to. Could I show you what I'm doing?

Maybe you could help me – I've started a business and I'm looking for the right person to work with – I know you are well-connected – could I show you what I am doing? If its not for you, you might know the right person for me to talk to.

I remember you saying…

I remember you were looking…

These last two are called "connectors" and they are very powerful as they show the person that you pay attention and that you truly feel that what you have is something that would want to learn about.

This isn't meant to tell *you* exactly what to say, just give you some fodder for you to consider.

Addendum 3 – Helping Others Solve Their Problems

Every successful business that exists solves someone's problem which is another way of saying that it meets their needs. It is the single reason why people purchase products and utilize services in life. A key part of helping someone solve their problems is for the person to understand and acknowledge that they have a problem to solve and that your products or business can solve it.

There are two basic approaches that can be used to help someone understand that what is available in your offer can solve someone's problem: Verbal persuasion and stories. I prefer to teach people how to properly tell stories, but before I explain that allow me to explain what is happening in a verbal persuasion approach.

Whenever we attempt to convince someone of something through verbal persuasion we do this using factual information and logic. The challenge is that we are explaining from our point of view and our information and logic, and the other person is listening through their own point of view based on their experiences and knowledge. Human beings by nature are self focused. We believe that our opinions are right, our actions are right, and what we know is right. Because we believe this we have an emotional interest in keeping things as we know them.

All people look at and listen to things from the perspective of "What's in it for me?" When we try to use logic and information to get people to buy-in to our way of thinking and seeing things, we are essentially trying to convince them that we are right. The other person therefore, must agree that we are right in order to take action on what we are telling them. The problem with this is that the other person must admit to themselves and to us, that their way of thinking about the topic is wrong.

The "What's in it for me?" thought process for the other person that we are trying to convince becomes holding onto their own beliefs. As a result they will be doing what is called "critical listening." This means instead of listening for how you could be right, they will be listening for any error in your logic that they can find based on what they already know. Since they will be basing this on what they know, they will be able to eventually find some reason to keep you wrong and them right.

The other person is emotionally invested in remaining right about their view of things. Only the best verbal persuaders are good enough to make a living in any field through this approach. It takes years of practice and study, and you must enjoy confrontation for this to become an area of expertise. It is not enjoyable for most people, including me.

Telling a story on the other hand creates an entirely different situation. Whenever someone hears a story, they again are creating their own image of the story in their mind. It is almost like they are watching a little movie in their head. By doing this the person naturally puts their favorite person, themselves, into the story. They are listening to our story as if it is happening to them.

This allows them to become emotionally involved in the story. They are not listening to the logic of the story; they are merely experiencing the story for themselves. Because they are participating emotionally in the story, they begin to think about how their life could be affected if what is going on in the story would happen to them.

Instead of thinking about how you could be wrong, they are thinking about how this story could be right for them. It allows them to ask you questions about how something could work for them instead of stating why they don't think it could be right for them.

The bottom line is this; anyone can learn to effectively communicate the benefits of a product or a business through a story. Its fun, it's easy, and allows others to more quickly see that what you have to offer can help them solve their problem. The key point of this is that when someone hears a story and begins to think that maybe this will solve their problem, they will pursue finding out how as if it was their idea. They will be emotionally invested in seeing how what you have to offer can help them. This is a fun way to do business and allows everyone to help more people.

Addendum 4 –
Health and Wellness

This is a bonus addendum for people working with Health and Wellness type products who are approaching for customers. All the same principles apply that you have read about so far, so these are just things that you can consider that are effective, as you are deciding what you want to say.

Have you heard about (your product) yet?

I have some great information about health and wellness. If I sent it to you would you listen to it?

You're interested in taking care of your health aren't you?

Are you open to ways to keep your family healthy?

Are you open to learning about new things to keep your family healthy?

Do you look for ways to keep yourself and your family healthy?

Are you interested in prevention?

I remember you saying you were dealing with....is that still bothering you?

If there was a way to help with _____ and it was safe and natural would you be open to learning about it?

The last time we talked you mentioned _____ is that still happening?

I'm using a product that is doing great things for me and I feel like I have a responsibility to let people know about it.

I started a wellness business from home with a great product and I wanted to let you know about it.

I started a wellness business from home and I would like to share some information with you.

I've started a business with a company whose products I've fallen in love with and I wanted to share the information with you.

I've started a wellness business and I'd like to be a resource for you and your family.

I found a great product for health and I feel a responsibility to share it.

I've discovered a product that…

I found a product that I love and I wanted to share it with you.

I've started a business where the main goal is to help people stay healthy, could I send you info about it?

I'm hoping you could help me. I've started a wellness business that's all about helping people stay healthy, could I send you some info/could we get together –if its not for you you might know someone I could help.

I have a story to tell you…

I gotta tell you what happened to me…

I gotta tell you what I found…

I have a product I'd like to run by you…

Addendum 5 – Network Marketing and Social Media

There is massive opportunity to build a business through social media and the internet. This growing frontier provides unique opportunities to work your business across the world from the comfort of your home.

The ability to work online expands the opportunity for everyone and is a catalyst for the growing home business revolution. You can now work your business at any hour of the day or night, and have mediums which allow you to grow into the skills that make it possible for someone to succeed regardless of their personality type.

The behaviors and the approaches do not change. You still conduct yourself with kindness, honesty and respect and no pressure. I teach people how to work effectively and efficiently online, but that is too large a scope for this little book.

There are however, some things to know right now to position yourself for when you do begin working online. Curiosity is important in attracting people to learn about what you are doing. Even though you are proud of your company and products, your online prospects do not know what you know. People want to learn as soon as they can. The minute you put your company name or product name on social media, you have lost control of the conversation. The prospect can now simply google to find out the information. This takes away your opportunity to talk to them about it.

Company web sites are typically well done and very professional. However, they are features based and do not tell the story the way you can. Features are all the background information. Benefits are what people are interested in. What is in it for them? Only if someone feels something will benefit them do they then care about the features.

In addition people look at things through their own level of experience. They will look at a company website to see how something is like something they already know. This will usually cause them to quickly make a decision that they already know about what you have, even though they don't.

So for now, make sure you do not post anything about your company or products on social media. In addition, do not put the name of your company on your profile. Learn how to properly use these platforms and then you can be effective with them.

Get Todd´s free training!

Sign up for Todd´s newsletter and get his free audio training "27 Phrases that Really Work in Prospecting for Your Home Business."

www.toddburrier.com

This is Todd's network marketing blog where he provides ongoing tips, education and podcasts.

@toddburrier.page

Order Todd´s books in EU or UK:

www.balance-tools.com

The Process 2

Maximum Efficiency and Results in Network Marketing

Enthusiasm and belief are the driving forces in network marketing and approach, information, follow up and serve are the core activities. This book will help you to be as effective as possible in these activities. Don´t let chance determine your success. This book provides answers to the most common challenges faced in the daily work of a networker.

➤ How to maximize your effectiveness when your time is limited

➤ Prioritize your work in the right way

➤ How to track your contacts for maximum results

➤ Open the right doors in your approaches

➤ Use your energy effectively and create momentum

➤ Transform your doubts

➤ How to provide outstanding service

➤ Leadership and soft skills

Leading with Heart

Powerful Wisdoms for Lasting Leadership in Network Marketing

This is an unprecedented time period in the Network Marketing industry. As of now, this industry is approaching $200 Billion in worldwide revenue and the growth rate has surpassed 6% annually the last 4 years. It has reached the point where it is no longer questioned as a viable way to create a long term income - and it's just getting started. Not only will more and more people be looking to this industry as the answer, but as technology continues to advance, the ability to build a network marketing business in minimal time per week across the world will get easier to do. But technology alone won't make you successful. Building a lasting residual income requires true leadership.

This book will guide you in becoming and remaining an authentic leader. Everything of value requires patience and persistence. Overcome the obstacles, master the challenges and develop your competency *and* your character. Authentic leadership is about helping others first and comes from the heart.

Let Todd inspire you with his special leadership style he has developed over many years. This book with the 44 powerful wisdoms is a must for every aspiring networker and leader.

Live Full live Well

Increase Joy, Fulfillment, and Productivity through Balance

"This is a work of passion for all the people who have sacrificed too much for far too little. It's never too late to change the way you live your life. It's for people who are trying to get it all done but know that every day is just not what it could be. This book is a real, honest, approach to life that can help anyone of any age to have more joy, fulfillment, and productivity in their life through the achievement of balance.

You are going to learn specifically how to develop a balanced lifestyle with this book. You will not read about work-life balance here, because I believe that *work-life balance is a misnomer.* To even acknowledge the idea of work-life balance is to say that work is equivalent to life. It is not. Life is bigger by miles. There are many aspects of your life that make up what you have to balance. Work happens to be one of them. Work is very important, but so are many other things. You will learn how to balance everything in a way that I have proven to work for over a decade. You will learn how to participate fully in the lives of your children and your spouse, your career, your personal wellbeing, the hobbies and causes you care about, the friendships that matter, and more." – Todd Burrier

The Blueprint Process for Building a long Term Successful Network Marketing Business from Scratch

In this program you will learn everything you need to build a solid foundation for a lasting network marketing business. Regardless of the system or style of your business this will serve you well. This a high value set of videos and bonuses that focus on the ideal ways to work with people, and will help you be more effective whether you are focusing on building off line or online.

www.toddburrier.com